Wine

Wine Record and Tasting Notes

Spruce Street Publishing
Toronto

Copyright © 1998 Spruce Street Publishing, Toronto

No part of this book may be reproduced in any form
or by any means without the express written permission
of the publisher.

Spruce Street Publishing
35D Spruce Street,
Toronto, Ontario M5A 2H8
(416) 922-6017

Canadian Cataloguing in Publication Data

Winger, Daniel M., 1960-
    Wine tasting journal: wine record and tasting notes

ISBN 0-9684366-0-9

    1. Wine tasting. I. Title.
TP548.5.A5W55 1998   641.2'2   C98-901380-4

Contents

◇

*F*ill ev'ry glass, for wine inspires us,

And fires us

With courage, love and joy.

John Gay
The Beggar's Opera

Introduction

Whether you are a connoisseur with an extensive wine cellar or a more modest wine drinker who simply enjoys sharing a bottle of wine at dinner, this journal will help you to develop your wine tasting skills and thereby enhance your appreciation of the subtle complexities of wine.

By taking the time to employ proper wine tasting techniques and making tasting notes in this journal you will have a permanent record of each wine tasting experience. This is invaluable for the serious wine collector who wants to carefully monitor the condition of his cellar - to record the subtle changes that develop over time and ensure that those fine reds are maturing as anticipated. But it is also useful for the casual wine drinker who wants a record of which wines have been purchased and which were found to be most enjoyable either alone or with food.

These notes can then be used to guide future wine selections and purchases as preferences for certain varieties, regions, or styles are developed.

The appreciation of wine is a passion that can be developed over a life time and is truly one of the great joys of life.

Cheers!

Wine Serving Considerations

◇ ───

Temperature - the temperature of a wine at serving has a very significant impact on how the wine will taste and how well it will be received by you and your guests. The typical rule of thumb for red wines is that they should be served at room temperature 65-68 degrees F (18-20 degrees C) and this is appropriate for most young Bordeaux but the age and weight of red wines may require slightly different serving temperatures. For example, a Beaujolais or other young, fruity, low tannin red wine would benefit by being served slightly chilled at a temperature of perhaps 54-58 degrees F (12-15 degrees C). On the other hand, a mature or old Bordeaux could be enhanced by serving at a temperature a degree or two higher than room temperature depending on the tannin levels and the overall quality of the wine.

White wines are generally served chilled or cold but again there is some variation in the optimal temperature for various types of white wines. Light, dry, acidic white wines should be served cold 45-50 degrees F (7-10 degrees C) as should sparkling wine. Full-bodied whites, particularly those aged in oak should be served chilled in the range of 50-54 degrees F (10-12 degrees C). White wines are usually placed in an ice bucket at the table in order to maintain the wines temperature. It is also a good idea to serve white wines half a glass at a time so that the wine does not warm too much in the glass before it is consumed.

It is important to experiment with tasting wines at different temperatures as the temperature of the wine has significant sensory effects. For example, at cold temperatures the aroma and bouquet tend to disappear and acidity and bitterness become more prominent. At very warm temperatures, the alcohol content is emphasized and the wine is perceived as heavier. As wine will inevitably tend to warm up in the glass it is often better to serve it on the cooler side - this applies to both reds and whites.

As a general rule you should find that the finer the wine the less chilling it will require and that lower quality wines benefit from being served on the cooler side as this tends to hide or mask the otherwise apparent faults.

Glassware - although there exists a large and specialized selection of crystal and glassware for consuming wines of various types and styles, for most red and white table wines all that is required is a clear, tulip shaped, stemmed glass of 6-10 ounces. The glass becomes an important tool in the process of "tasting" a wine as opposed to simply drinking it. Good quality glass or crystal allows us to fully appreciate the colour and clarity of the wine as well as its viscosity or "legs". The tulip shape of the bowl helps to both release and capture the aromas of the wine which is an essential component of the tasting experience. The long stem of the wine glass helps to keep the wine at the proper temperature as long as the glass is held by the stem and not the bowl.

One general custom regarding wine glasses is that for red wines the size of the bowl tends to be larger and the amount of taper to the opening tends to be somewhat less when compared to a typical glass for white wine. This difference is due to the more volatile, complex and intense nature of the aroma molecules of red wines and because the release of the aroma or bouquet is considered a more vital component of the tasting and enjoyment of red wines.

As a result a typical serving glass for a red wine such as a Pinot Noir has a large bowl which provides ample surface area for swirling the wine and for evaporation which release the wines aroma. The space between the surface of the wine in the glass and the top of the glass is also relatively large which allows the aromas to circulate, develop and concentrate. The rim of the glass is slightly tapered inward to achieve a balance of containing the aromas in the bowl and allowing them to escape. On the other hand, a typical white wine would probably be better served in a smaller wine glass with more taper to the rim to hold in and concentrate the more subtle aromas. In either case the wine glass should only be filled to about one-third full to allow space to capture the aroma.

Decanting - the decanting of a wine is necessary only if there is a considerable amount of sediment in the wine bottle as this can effect both the appearance and the taste of the wine. This is best done by allowing the bottle to stand upright until all of the sediment has settled to the bottom. The wine can then be slowly and carefully poured into a wine decanter or other serving container. A strong light or candle held at the neck of the bottle will assist in monitoring the flow of wine and assure that the sediment and dregs remain in the wine bottle. As a general rule only older reds and vintage port will throw off a sediment, however sometimes a white wine will throw off a sediment of whitish tartrate crystals. Although these crystals are quite harmless, you may wish to decant these wines as well.

Other reasons for decanting could be to aerate the wine prior to serving which can greatly benefit young red wines or simply for purposes of presentation, that is, to show the wine off in a cut crystal decanter or carafe.

Other Considerations - some other things to consider when serving wine is whether the wine should be allowed to "breathe" before serving; how to determine if the wine is off or "corked"; and the order of serving wines over the course of a dinner.

Although opinions vary, the act of opening a bottle of wine and letting it sit prior to serving will have very little effect or benefit on the taste of the wine. The amount of aeration that can occur through the narrow neck of a wine bottle is minimal and in fact the act of pouring the wine into a glass or decanting the wine will have a much greater and immediate effect. After pouring, the wine will continue to develop and "open up" in the glass as it is swirled and exposed to the air while drinking.

When ordering wine in a restaurant, the server will usually present you with the cork and a small sample of the wine to examine upon opening. This is your opportunity to determine whether the wine is fit to drink, that is, whether or not the wine is spoiled or "corked". The best way to determine this is by smelling both the end of the cork and the wine for signs of strong musty or moldy odours. If the wine is spoiled these odours will be very apparent. If there are no traces of "off" smells the wine should then be examined for clarity. A cloudiness or flatness in colour may also indicate that there is a problem with the wine. Finally, the wine should be tasted and assessed not for quality but only for determining whether there are any signs of spoilage. Simply being unhappy with your selection is not grounds for returning the bottle.

Although the incidence of purchasing a spoiled bottle of wine is quite low, the above ritual should still be employed both in a restaurant and at home to avoid the embarrassment of serving your dinner companions a spoiled glass of wine.

Finally, the general rule or custom when serving a variety of wines over the course of a meal is to serve; white wines before red wines, dry wines before sweet, and light bodied before full-bodied. The dictum being, "the bottle being drunk should never make one regret the one that has just been drunk".

Wine Tasting Techniques

Following is a description of the various steps and techniques that one should take when assessing and tasting a wine - the outcome of which will form the basis of your tasting notes.

Appearance - Colour, Clarity, & Viscosity

Colour/Hue and Clarity - the first step in assessing a wine, after being poured in an appropriate glass, is by its appearance or more precisely by noting its colour or hue and its clarity.

Colour can reveal a considerable amount of information about a wine and is in fact one of the best ways of assessing the age or maturity of a wine in a blind tasting. White wines get deeper and darker in colour as they age and oxidize while reds actually get paler and lighter with age as the pigments settle out or precipitate forming part of the sediment.

Colour can vary in intensity from very pale to deep. White wines can vary from very pale yellow tinted with green through to straw and golden-yellows and amber. The range of colour for reds run from deep purple and garnet fading through to dark-red, ruby, crimson, mahogany, and brick.

To properly observe the colour of a wine the glass should be held at a 45 degree angle against a white background (white napkin or table-cloth) and with a sufficient source of light. By tilting the glass it is possible to observe the nuance of hue from the centre of the bowl to the edge or rim, this is particularly evident in red wines. The principal colour of the wine is the colour observed in the bowl and is the result of numerous factors not the least of which are the grape variety, the climate, the amount of extract during fermentation, ageing in oak, and overall quality of the vintage. The rim extends from the watery edge to the main body of colour in the bowl and may only be one-eighth of an inch wide in a very young concentrated wine to over one-half inch wide in a light bodied or mature wine. In red wines the colour at the rim will give a further indication of maturity. In young wines it will still be purplish or violet but as the wine ages the rim will become wider, paler and increasingly red-brown to brick coloured with tints of mahogany, orange or amber.

To assess the clarity and depth of a wine the glass should be held up to a light source and viewed from above. Generally, we would expect the wine to be clear and bright, however, some wines may appear a little dull or muddy which in most cases would be considered a fault. Some of the finest wines will have a quality distinct from brightness which can best be described as luminescence, brilliance or opulence.

Viscosity - another consideration when judging a wines appearance is its viscosity or "legs". After swirling the glass some of the wine will cling to the sides and gather together to form droplets which then run back down the sides forming "arches" or "tears". The heavier or more viscous the wine, the more of these "tears" there will be and the longer it will take for them to form. This is indicative of the alcohol content and/or the residual sugar content of the wine but is not the best guide to the wines weight or body because how the "tears" form can be equally affected by the surface, shape and cleanliness of the glass. The best judge of the weight of a wine is the palate.

Nose - Aroma & Bouquet

Aroma/**Bouquet** - although sometimes used interchangeably, strictly speaking the aroma refers to the smells attributable primarily to the grape variety as well as such things as the soil conditions, and the fermentation and ageing process prior to bottling, while the bouquet most often refers to those more complex and subtle aromas that are attributable to fine wines and develop for the most part in the bottle. Therefore, for most wines the term aroma is often most appropriate.

To release the aroma it is customary to swirl the wine in the glass either with the base flat on the table or in the air holding the glass by the stem. This action aerates the wine and helps to release the volatile molecules into the air in the upper portion of the glass. The glass is then lifted to the nose at about 45 degrees and the aromas are inhaled and noted. Holding the nostrils close to the lower rim of the glass aids in detecting the heavier or headier characteristics while at the upper rim of the glass the more delicate and subtle aspects are more easily distinguished. Another interesting technique is using alternate nostrils to get at or distinguish the aromas. To do this, tilt both the head and the glass to favour one or the other nostril.

Describing the olfactory sensations attributable to wine is difficult to say the least, although the primary varietal aroma can usually be quite easily identified. For example, most Cabernet Sauvignon have a distinct "blackcurrant" characteristic while a Merlot is often described as "buttery". Ageing in new oak can also produce common aromas such as "vanilla" or other "spicy" or "woody" aromas.

Other aromas are much more difficult and subjective. The most common smell categories used to identify wine aromas are: floral, fruity, spicy, animal, vegetal, and mineral . Within these broad categories are an almost unlimited number of more precise descriptions or comparisons. For example, a wine with a floral nose may be compared to "violets" or perhaps "rose petals", a wine with a fruity nose could smell of "citrus" or "apricot" or "green apple" depending both on the wine and the subjective interpretation of the taster.

As you gain experience tasting wines and making tasting notes you will develop descriptive comparisons and terminology for the variety and intensity of aromas that you will encounter.

Palate - Texture, Taste, Finish & Balance

Texture/**Mouthfeel** - these sensations on the palate are related to the sensation of touch and include astringency, body, temperature and texture. Astringency is the mouth puckering or drying sensation most often attributed to the level of tannins in red wines or that could also be caused by high levels of acidity. The body or weight of a wine is primarily a function of the alcohol content. A light wine being relatively low in alcohol as compared to a medium, heavy or full-bodied wine. However, other factors such as the intensity of flavours, the density and the overall balance of the wine are also important when describing body. Generally, any "watery" quality in the wine would denote a lack of body.

Temperature, as discussed earlier, plays an important role in the way a wine "feels". It can modify for better or worse the effects of alcohol, tannin and acidity. Texture refers to the overall feel and consistency of the wine on the palate. Most descriptions of texture use visual and tactile analogies, such as smooth, polished, granular, hard, soft, coarse, silky or velvety.

Taste, **Finish and Balance** - when initially tasting a wine for the purposes of making a tasting note, it is best to take a relatively small sip of wine - a little more than a tablespoon. The wine should then be gently worked around the mouth from side to side and around to the back of the tongue. A little wine could be swallowed during this process. To enhance the flavours and to fully analyse the constitution of the wine it is necessary to draw in a little air through the wine to help release its volatile components. This action will bring forward the acid, tannin, alcohol and flavour components of the wine. It takes some practice to do this proficiently and if done properly will create a pronounced slurping sound. All or a portion of the remaining wine could now be swallowed with any balance being spit or worked in the mouth again. The wine should be held in the mouth for at most about 20-25 seconds and obviously should only be spat out if at a formal wine tasting where this is the custom.

After the final swallow, breathe out through the nose and mouth and smack the lips and palate to assess the finish and aftertaste. The finish comprises all of the sensations of taste, texture and aroma. The aftertaste refers to just the sensations of taste and aroma which persist or linger after swallowing. Thus the aftertaste is the final component of the finish. The term "length" is used to describe how long all the sensations of the finish last.

When tasting a wine one should look for and record the initial sensations or "attack" on the palate. Whether it is soft or firm, as well as how soon signs of acidity or tannins appear. Next comes the development of the wine on the palate as the wine is worked in the mouth. An assessment of the flavours and aromatics for both character and intensity as well as how long they are sustained and the quality of the texture. Lastly, the characteristics of the finish are noted. These are the final impressions of the texture, and the length and balance of flavours and aromas in the aftertaste.

Once the characteristics of the texture, taste and finish of the wine have been noted one can make an assessment of the overall balance of the wine. The term balance implies neither a deficit or excess of any one component and is specific to the style and origin of the wine. Therefore, what you are looking for is an overall balance of acid, alcohol, tannin, sugar, and flavours that is consistent with the style of wine being tasted. It is important to remember that what constitutes good balance varies from region to region and grape to grape. As balance is a more qualitative assessment it can take considerable tasting experience to fully evaluate, but when a wine is harmoniously balanced it is apparent and appreciated by even the most novice of wine drinkers.

The elements of taste include sweetness/dryness, acidity, alcohol, tannin, fruit, wood and other flavours. The first thing noticed when tasting a wine is often its level of sweetness. This is particularly true of white wines as most quality red wines are dry with virtually no residual sugar. A wine that is very dry would be totally lacking in sweetness, wines could also be described as dry, semi-dry, slightly sweet or sweet. Wines with naturally high acidity need a certain amount of sweetness to achieve balance on the palate.

A certain level of acidity can produce a refreshing quality by balancing sweetness, it also adds length to the finish of a wine. To little acidity and the wine might be described as flat or shapeless, too much and the wine may taste sharp, tart, green or unripe. A wine with an appropriate level of acidity could be described as crisp, clean, fresh, or even mouthwatering.

The alcohol level of a wine is "felt" on the palate rather than tasted and is perceived in terms of weight, body or warmth. It is difficult to separate the perception of alcohol from other qualities such as depth of flavour and texture and therefore we might use descriptions such as watery or weak if there is a lack of alcohol. Too much alcohol and the wine might be described as heavy or hot. Generally, the terms light, medium, and full-bodied are used to note the alcohol content of a wine.

Tannin is derived from grape skins during fermentation and like alcohol is perceived more as a texture than a taste. Tannin has a drying quality in the mouth and in young wines can produce a bitter or tinny taste as well. A wine with a substantial tannic content also requires high alcohol to achieve balance.

Wines may be described as lightly, moderately or very tannic and can produce qualities ranging from supple, firm, rich and chewy to tough, coarse and bitter.

The acid, alcohol and tannin content provides the backbone of a wine which supports the other more complex, subtle and interesting flavours that are attributable to the grape variety, the soil and climate conditions, fermentation, and the other biochemical processes that occur during aging. Most people relate a wines flavour by analogy to other taste experiences or impressions. Comparison to various fruit flavours such as apricot, apple, blackcurrent, cherry, citrus, kiwi, melon, peach, pear or plum are common. Spice flavours such as anise, clove, cinnamon, nutmeg, pepper and vanilla might also be detected. Other impressions of taste are derived from comparison to minerals or soil conditions and include; chalk, earth, flint, gravel, oil, and tar. Other common tastes are; butter, caramel, cedar, chocolate, coffee, honey, mint, nutty, oak, smoke, toast and yeast.

The complex and subtle taste and flavour of wine is part of its challenge and mystery. Developing the ability to discern and put into words these characteristics is well worth the effort.

Overall Assessment - this section of the tasting note is designed for more encompassing, qualitative comments and can also reflect the tasters personal preferences. It can also include comments on whether the wine is ready to drink and its prospects for further improvement in the future.

Descriptive Terms

Appearance

Colour/Hue: amber, brick, brownish, burgundy, cranberry, crimson, garnet, greenish, golden, honeyed, lemon, magenta, mahogany, mauve, orange, plum, purple, red, rose, ruby, ruddy, straw, tawny, violet, yellow

Clarity: bitty, bright, brilliant, clear, cloudy, crystal, dark, dense, deep, dull, effervescent, hazy, inky, iridescent, lustrous, muddy, murky, opulent, pale, rich, sunny, warm

Nose

Aroma/Bouquet: almond, bold, burnt, butterscotch, buttery, cherry, chocolate, cinnamon, citrus, clean, corked, earthy, floral, fresh, fruity, full, funky, gooseberry, grapey, grapefruit, grassy, green/unripe, hay, honey, honeysuckle, leather, lemon, lime, lively, mushroom, musky, oaky, passionfruit, peppery, perfumed, pineapple, pine, powerful, raisin, raspberry, resin, rich, ripe, rose petal, spicy, subtle, sulphur, tar, toasty, tobacco, tropical, vibrant, violet, woody, yeasty

Palate

Texture/Mouthfeel: acid, aggressive, astringent, bold, cool, concentrated, creamy, crisp, dry, dense, fine, fleshy, fresh, generous, gentle, gritty, hot, juicy, lush, meaty, mouthfilling, oily, plump, puckering, refined, rich, silky, smooth, soft, supple, tannic, tough, velvety, watery

Taste: anise, apple, berry, burnt toast, caramel, cassis, cedar, ripe cherry, sour cherry, chocolate, citrus, clove, coconut, coffee, earthy, flinty, fruity, gamey, grapey, grapefruit, kiwi, lemon, licorice, melon, mineral, mint, mulberry, nutmeg, nutty, oak, oil, orange, peach, pear, pepper, pineapple, plum, prune, raisin, red currant, ripe fruit, rhubarb, savoury, smoky, sour, spicy, sweet, tar, tangerine, vanilla

Finish: acidic, clean, cloying, crisp, delicate, dry, drying, fine, firm, flat, full, hard, lean, lingering, long, mellow, pleasant, seamless, short, slippery, subtle, tannic, tough, velvety

Balance: acidic, coarse, complex, delicate, developed, edgy, elegant, excellent, full, full-bodied, generous, harmonious, heavy, immature, integrated, lean, light, light-weight/body, mature, medium-weight/body, mouthfilling, over-oxidized, robust, round, smooth, soft, thin, well-balanced, well-rounded, well-structured, young

Wine Record and Tasting Notes

◇

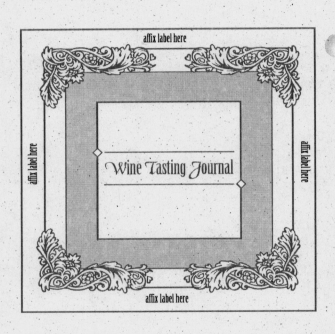

affix label here

affix label here

affix label here

Wine Tasting Journal

affix label here

Wine Record

◇

Name: _____

Producer: _____

Importer: _____

Grape Variety(ies): _____

Style/Region: _____ Vintage: _____

Date Purchased: _____ Country: _____

Purchase Price: _____ No. of bottles: _____

Purchased from: _____

Tasting Note

◇

Date opened: _____

Served with: _____

Guests: _____

Colour/Hue, Clarity: _____

_____

Aroma/Bouquet: _____

_____

Texture, Taste, Finish, Balance: _____

_____

Overall Assessment: _____

_____

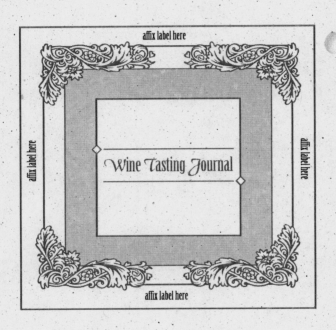

affix label here

affix label here

affix label here

Wine Tasting Journal

affix label here

Wine Record

Name: _____

Producer: _____

Importer: _____

Grape Variety(ies): _____

Style/Region: _____ Vintage: _____

Date Purchased: _____ Country: _____

Purchase Price: _____ No. of bottles: _____

Purchased from: _____

Tasting Note

Date opened: _____

Served with: _____

Guests: _____

Colour/Hue, Clarity: _____

_____

Aroma/Bouquet: _____

_____

Texture, Taste, Finish, Balance: _____

_____

Overall Assessment: _____

_____

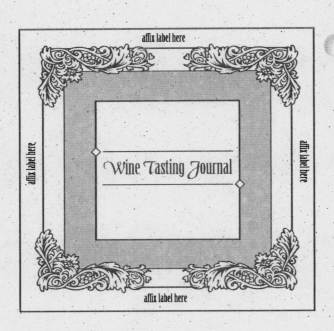

affix label here

affix label here

affix label here

affix label here

Wine Tasting Journal

Wine Record

◇

Name: _____

Producer: _____

Importer: _____

Grape Variety(ies): _____

Style/Region: _____ Vintage: _____

Date Purchased: _____ Country: _____

Purchase Price: _____ No. of bottles: _____

Purchased from: _____

Tasting Note

◇

Date opened: _____

Served with: _____

Guests: _____

Colour/Hue, Clarity: _____

_____

Aroma/Bouquet: _____

_____

Texture, Taste, Finish, Balance: _____

_____

Overall Assessment: _____

_____

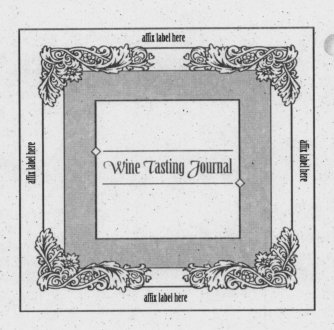

affix label here

affix label here

affix label here

affix label here

Wine Tasting Journal

Wine Record

Name: _____

Producer: _____

Importer: _____

Grape Variety(ies): _____

Style/Region: _____ Vintage: _____

Date Purchased: _____ Country: _____

Purchase Price: _____ No. of bottles: _____

Purchased from: _____

Tasting Note

Date opened: _____

Served with: _____

Guests: _____

Colour/Hue, Clarity: _____

_____

Aroma/Bouquet: _____

_____

Texture, Taste, Finish, Balance: _____

_____

Overall Assessment: _____

_____

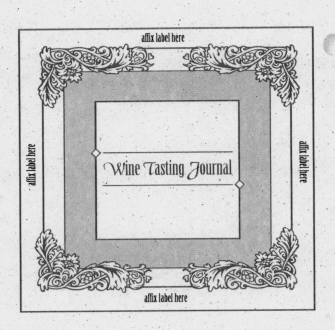

affix label here

affix label here

affix label here

affix label here

Wine Tasting Journal

Wine Record

Name: _____

Producer: _____

Importer: _____

Grape Variety(ies): _____

Style/Region: _____ Vintage: _____

Date Purchased: _____ Country: _____

Purchase Price: _____ No. of bottles: _____

Purchased from: _____

Tasting Note

Date opened: _____

Served with: _____

Guests: _____

Colour/Hue, Clarity: _____

_____

Aroma/Bouquet: _____

_____

Texture, Taste, Finish, Balance: _____

_____

Overall Assessment: _____

_____

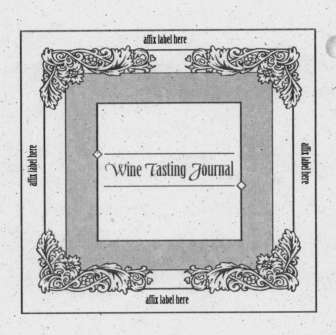

affix label here

affix label here

affix label here

affix label here

Wine Tasting Journal

Wine Record

◇

Name: _____

Producer: _____

Importer: _____

Grape Variety(ies): _____

Style/Region: _____ Vintage: _____

Date Purchased: _____ Country: _____

Purchase Price: _____ No. of bottles: _____

Purchased from: _____

Tasting Note

◇

Date opened: _____

Served with: _____

Guests: _____

Colour/Hue, Clarity: _____

_____

Aroma/Bouquet: _____

_____

Texture, Taste, Finish, Balance: _____

_____

Overall Assessment: _____

_____

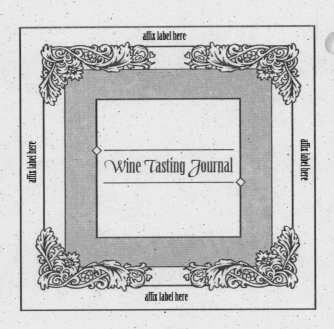

affix label here

affix label here

affix label here

Wine Tasting Journal

affix label here

Wine Record

◇

Name: _____

Producer: _____

Importer: _____

Grape Variety(ies): _____

Style/Region: _____ Vintage: _____

Date Purchased: _____ Country: _____

Purchase Price: _____ No. of bottles: _____

Purchased from: _____

Tasting Note

◇

Date opened: _____

Served with: _____

Guests: _____

Colour/Hue, Clarity: _____

_____

Aroma/Bouquet: _____

_____

Texture, Taste, Finish, Balance: _____

_____

Overall Assessment: _____

_____

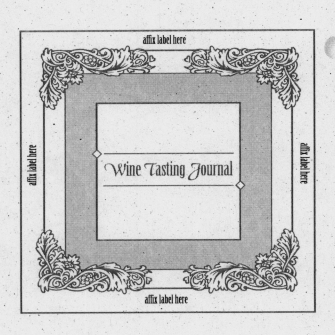

affix label here

affix label here

affix label here

affix label here

Wine Tasting Journal

Wine Record

Name: _____

Producer: _____

Importer: _____

Grape Variety(ies): _____

Style/Region: _____ Vintage: _____

Date Purchased: _____ Country: _____

Purchase Price: _____ No. of bottles: _____

Purchased from: _____

Tasting Note

Date opened: _____

Served with: _____

Guests: _____

Colour/Hue, Clarity: _____

_____

Aroma/Bouquet: _____

_____

Texture, Taste, Finish, Balance: _____

_____

Overall Assessment: _____

_____

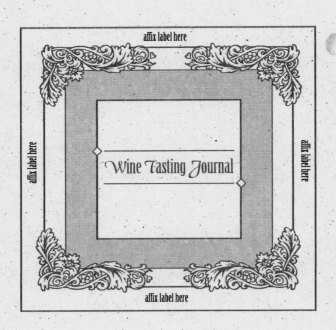

affix label here

affix label here

affix label here

Wine Tasting Journal

affix label here

Wine Record ◇

Name: _____

Producer: _____

Importer: _____

Grape Variety(ies): _____

Style/Region: _____ Vintage: _____

Date Purchased: _____ Country: _____

Purchase Price: _____ No. of bottles: _____

Purchased from: _____

Tasting Note ◇

Date opened: _____

Served with: _____

Guests: _____

Colour/Hue, Clarity: _____

_____

Aroma/Bouquet: _____

_____

Texture, Taste, Finish, Balance: _____

_____

Overall Assessment: _____

_____

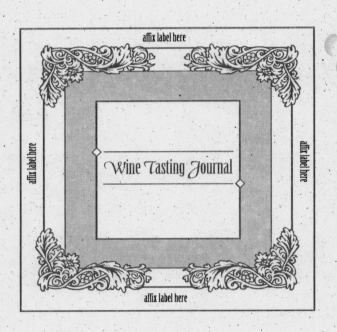

affix label here

affix label here

affix label here

affix label here

Wine Tasting Journal

Wine Record

Name: _____

Producer: _____

Importer: _____

Grape Variety(ies): _____

Style/Region: _____ Vintage: _____

Date Purchased: _____ Country: _____

Purchase Price: _____ No. of bottles: _____

Purchased from: _____

Tasting Note

Date opened: _____

Served with: _____

Guests: _____

Colour/Hue, Clarity: _____

_____

Aroma/Bouquet: _____

_____

Texture, Taste, Finish, Balance: _____

_____

Overall Assessment: _____

_____

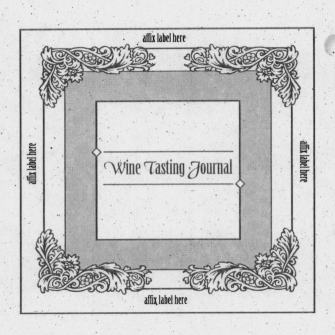

affix label here

affix label here

affix label here

affix label here

Wine Tasting Journal

Wine Record ◇

Name: _____

Producer: _____

Importer: _____

Grape Variety(ies): _____

Style/Region: _____ Vintage: _____

Date Purchased: _____ Country: _____

Purchase Price: _____ No. of bottles: _____

Purchased from: _____

Tasting Note ◇

Date opened: _____

Served with: _____

Guests: _____

Colour/Hue, Clarity: _____

_____

Aroma/Bouquet: _____

_____

Texture, Taste, Finish, Balance: _____

_____

Overall Assessment: _____

_____

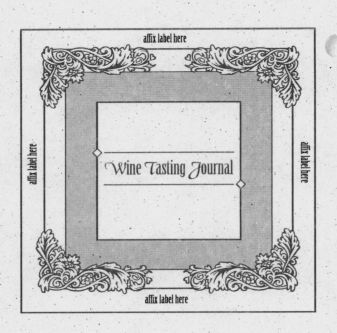

affix label here

affix label here

affix label here

affix label here

Wine Tasting Journal

Wine Record

Name: _____

Producer: _____

Importer: _____

Grape Variety(ies): _____

Style/Region: _____ _____ Vintage: _____

Date Purchased: _____ Country: _____

Purchase Price: _____ No. of bottles: _____

Purchased from: _____

Tasting Note

Date opened: _____

Served with: _____

Guests: _____

Colour/Hue, Clarity: _____

_____

Aroma/Bouquet: _____

_____

Texture, Taste, Finish, Balance: _____

_____

Overall Assessment: _____

_____

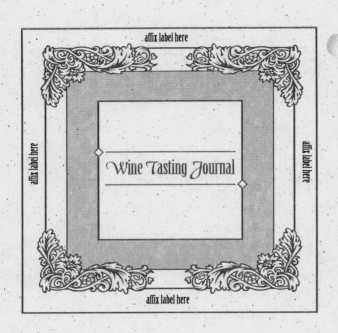

affix label here

affix label here

Wine Tasting Journal

affix label here

affix label here

Wine Record

◇

Name: _____

Producer: _____

Importer: _____

Grape Variety(ies): _____

Style/Region: _____ Vintage: _____

Date Purchased: _____ Country: _____

Purchase Price: _____ No. of bottles: _____

Purchased from: _____

Tasting Note

◇

Date opened: _____

Served with: _____

Guests: _____

Colour/Hue, Clarity: _____

_____

Aroma/Bouquet: _____

_____

Texture, Taste, Finish, Balance: _____

_____

Overall Assessment: _____

_____

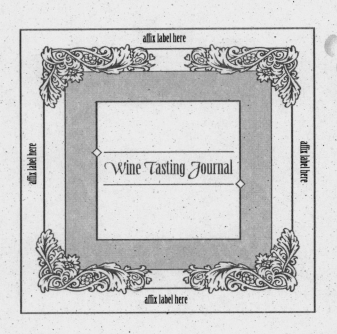

affix label here

affix label here

affix label here

affix label here

Wine Tasting Journal

Wine Record

◇

Name: _____

Producer: _____

Importer: _____

Grape Variety(ies): _____

Style/Region: _____ Vintage: _____

Date Purchased: _____ Country: _____

Purchase Price: _____ No. of bottles: _____

Purchased from: _____

Tasting Note

◇

Date opened: _____

Served with: _____

Guests: _____

Colour/Hue, Clarity: _____

_____

Aroma/Bouquet: _____

_____

Texture, Taste, Finish, Balance: _____

_____

Overall Assessment: _____

_____

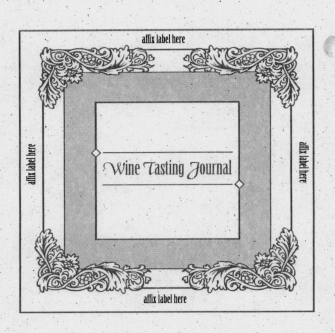

affix label here

affix label here

affix label here

affix label here

Wine Tasting Journal

Wine Record

◇

Name: _____

Producer: _____

Importer: _____

Grape Variety(ies): _____

Style/Region: _____ Vintage: _____

Date Purchased: _____ Country: _____

Purchase Price: _____ No. of bottles: _____

Purchased from: _____

Tasting Note

◇

Date opened: _____

Served with: _____

Guests: _____

Colour/Hue, Clarity: _____

_____

Aroma/Bouquet: _____

_____

Texture, Taste, Finish, Balance: _____

_____

Overall Assessment: _____

_____

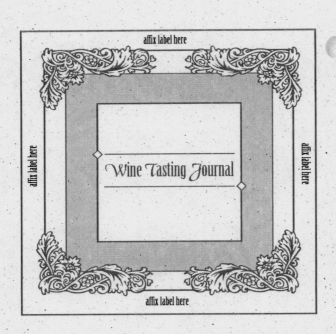

affix label here

affix label here

affix label here

affix label here

Wine Tasting Journal

Wine Record

◇

Name: _____

Producer: _____

Importer: _____

Grape Variety(ies): _____

Style/Region: _____ Vintage: _____

Date Purchased: _____ Country: _____

Purchase Price: _____ No. of bottles: _____

Purchased from: _____

Tasting Note

◇

Date opened: _____

Served with: _____

Guests: _____

Colour/Hue, Clarity: _____

_____

Aroma/Bouquet: _____

_____

Texture, Taste, Finish, Balance: _____

_____

Overall Assessment: _____

_____

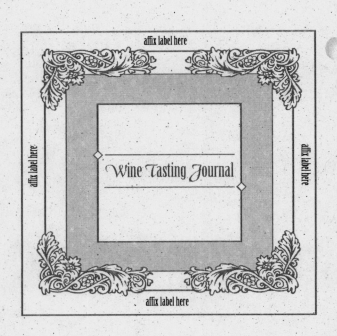

affix label here

affix label here

affix label here

Wine Tasting Journal

affix label here

Wine Record ◇

Name: _____

Producer: _____

Importer: _____

Grape Variety(ies): _____

Style/Region: _____ Vintage: _____

Date Purchased: _____ Country: _____

Purchase Price: _____ No. of bottles: _____

Purchased from: _____

Tasting Note ◇

Date opened: _____

Served with: _____

Guests: _____

Colour/Hue, Clarity: _____

_____

Aroma/Bouquet: _____

_____

Texture, Taste, Finish, Balance: _____

_____

Overall Assessment: _____

_____

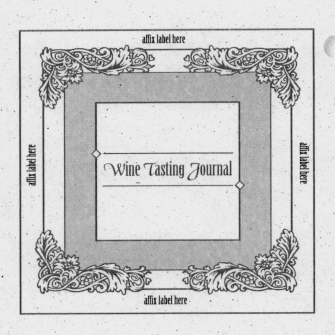

affix label here

affix label here

affix label here

Wine Tasting Journal

affix label here

Wine Record

◇

Name: _____

Producer: _____

Importer: _____

Grape Variety(ies): _____

Style/Region: _____ Vintage: _____

Date Purchased: _____ Country: _____

Purchase Price: _____ No. of bottles: _____

Purchased from: _____

Tasting Note

◇

Date opened: _____

Served with: _____

Guests: _____

Colour/Hue, Clarity: _____

_____

Aroma/Bouquet: _____

_____

Texture, Taste, Finish, Balance: _____

_____

Overall Assessment: _____

_____

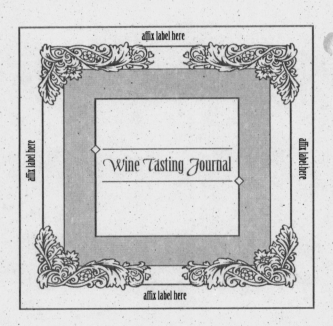

affix label here

affix label here

affix label here

Wine Tasting Journal

affix label here

Wine Record

Name: _____

Producer: _____

Importer: _____

Grape Variety(ies): _____

Style/Region: _____ Vintage: _____

Date Purchased: _____ Country: _____

Purchase Price: _____ No. of bottles: _____

Purchased from: _____

Tasting Note

Date opened: _____

Served with: _____

Guests: _____

Colour/Hue, Clarity: _____

_____

Aroma/Bouquet: _____

_____

Texture, Taste, Finish, Balance: _____

_____

Overall Assessment: _____

_____

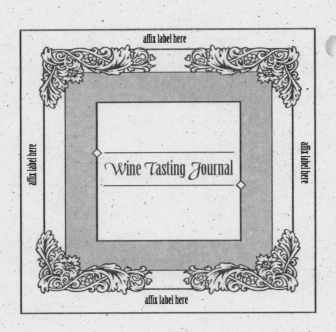

affix label here

affix label here

affix label here

Wine Tasting Journal

affix label here

Wine Record

◇

Name: _____

Producer: _____

Importer: _____

Grape Variety(ies): _____

Style/Region: _____ Vintage: _____

Date Purchased: _____ Country: _____

Purchase Price: _____ No. of bottles: _____

Purchased from: _____

Tasting Note

◇

Date opened: _____

Served with: _____

Guests: _____

Colour/Hue, Clarity: _____

_____

Aroma/Bouquet: _____

_____

Texture, Taste, Finish, Balance: _____

_____

Overall Assessment: _____

_____

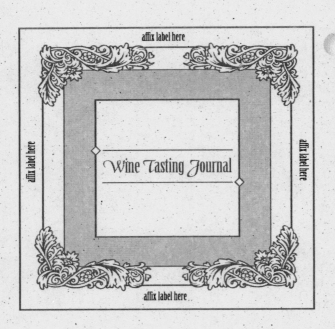

affix label here

affix label here

affix label here

Wine Tasting Journal

affix label here

Wine Record

Name: _____

Producer: _____

Importer: _____

Grape Variety(ies): _____

Style/Region: _____ Vintage: _____

Date Purchased: _____ Country: _____

Purchase Price: _____ No. of bottles: _____

Purchased from: _____

Tasting Note

Date opened: _____

Served with: _____

Guests: _____

Colour/Hue, Clarity: _____

_____

Aroma/Bouquet: _____

_____

Texture, Taste, Finish, Balance: _____

_____

Overall Assessment: _____

_____

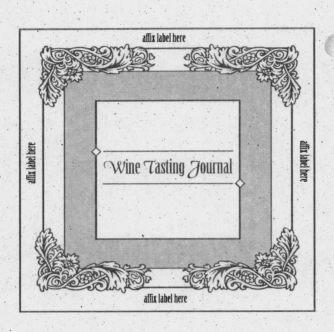

affix label here

affix label here

affix label here

affix label here

Wine Tasting Journal

Wine Record ◇

Name: _____

Producer: _____

Importer: _____

Grape Variety(ies): _____

Style/Region: _____ Vintage: _____

Date Purchased: _____ Country: _____

Purchase Price: _____ No. of bottles: _____

Purchased from: _____

Tasting Note ◇

Date opened: _____

Served with: _____

Guests: _____

Colour/Hue, Clarity: _____

_____

Aroma/Bouquet: _____

_____

Texture, Taste, Finish, Balance: _____

_____

Overall Assessment: _____

_____

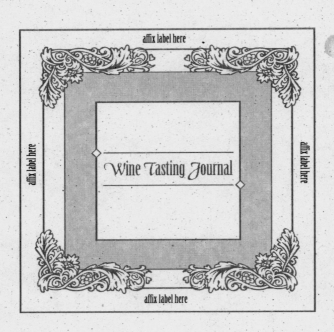

affix label here

affix label here

affix label here

affix label here

Wine Tasting Journal

Wine Record

◇

Name: _____

Producer: _____

Importer: _____

Grape Variety(ies): _____

Style/Region: _____ Vintage: _____

Date Purchased: _____ Country: _____

Purchase Price: _____ No. of bottles: _____

Purchased from: _____

Tasting Note

◇

Date opened: _____

Served with: _____

Guests: _____

Colour/Hue, Clarity: _____

_____

Aroma/Bouquet: _____

_____

Texture, Taste, Finish, Balance: _____

_____

Overall Assessment: _____

_____

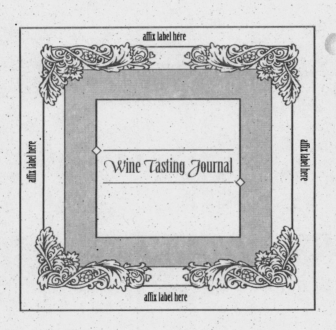

affix label here

affix label here

affix label here

affix label here

Wine Tasting Journal

Wine Record

Name: _____

Producer: _____

Importer: _____

Grape Variety(ies): _____

Style/Region: _____ Vintage: _____

Date Purchased: _____ Country: _____

Purchase Price: _____ No. of bottles: _____

Purchased from: _____

Tasting Note

Date opened: _____

Served with: _____

Guests: _____

Colour/Hue, Clarity: _____

_____

Aroma/Bouquet: _____

_____

Texture, Taste, Finish, Balance: _____

_____

Overall Assessment: _____

_____

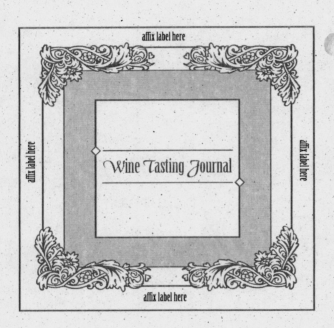

affix label here

affix label here

affix label here

Wine Tasting Journal

affix label here

Wine Record ◇

Name: _____

Producer: _____

Importer: _____

Grape Variety(ies): _____

Style/Region: _____ Vintage: _____

Date Purchased: _____ Country: _____

Purchase Price: _____ No. of bottles: _____

Purchased from: _____

Tasting Note ◇

Date opened: _____

Served with: _____

Guests: _____

Colour/Hue, Clarity: _____

_____

Aroma/Bouquet: _____

_____

Texture, Taste, Finish, Balance: _____

_____

Overall Assessment: _____

_____

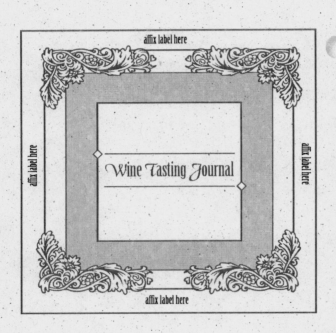

affix label here

affix label here

affix label here

Wine Tasting Journal

affix label here

Wine Record

◇

Name: _____

Producer: _____

Importer: _____

Grape Variety(ies): _____

Style/Region: _____ Vintage: _____

Date Purchased: _____ Country: _____

Purchase Price: _____ No. of bottles: _____

Purchased from: _____

Tasting Note

◇

Date opened: _____

Served with: _____

Guests: _____

Colour/Hue, Clarity: _____

_____

Aroma/Bouquet: _____

_____

Texture, Taste, Finish, Balance: _____

_____

Overall Assessment: _____

_____

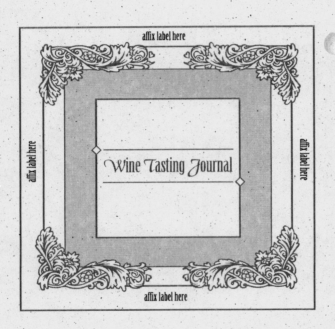

affix label here

affix label here

affix label here

Wine Tasting Journal

affix label here

Wine Record

◇

Name: _____

Producer: _____

Importer: _____

Grape Variety(ies): _____

Style/Region: _____ Vintage: _____

Date Purchased: _____ Country: _____

Purchase Price: _____ No. of bottles: _____

Purchased from: _____

Tasting Note

◇

Date opened: _____

Served with: _____

Guests: _____

Colour/Hue, Clarity: _____

_____

Aroma/Bouquet: _____

_____

Texture, Taste, Finish, Balance: _____

_____

Overall Assessment: _____

_____

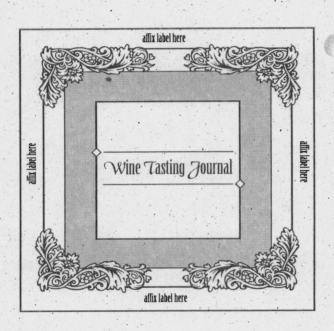

affix label here

affix label here

affix label here

Wine Tasting Journal

affix label here

Wine Record

◇

Name: _____

Producer: _____

Importer: _____

Grape Variety(ies): _____

Style/Region: _____ Vintage: _____

Date Purchased: _____ Country: _____

Purchase Price: _____ No. of bottles: _____

Purchased from: _____

Tasting Note

◇

Date opened: _____

Served with: _____

Guests: _____

Colour/Hue, Clarity: _____

_____

Aroma/Bouquet: _____

_____

Texture, Taste, Finish, Balance: _____

_____

Overall Assessment: _____

_____

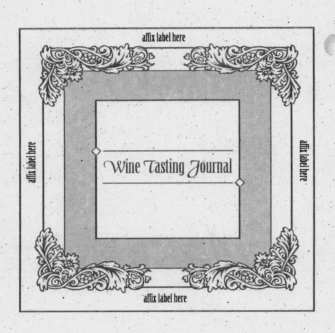

affix label here

affix label here

affix label here

affix label here

Wine Tasting Journal

Wine Record

◇

Name: _____

Producer: _____

Importer: _____

Grape Variety(ies): _____

Style/Region: _____ Vintage: _____

Date Purchased: _____ Country: _____

Purchase Price: _____ No. of bottles: _____

Purchased from: _____

Tasting Note

◇

Date opened: _____

Served with: _____

Guests: _____

Colour/Hue, Clarity: _____

_____

Aroma/Bouquet: _____

_____

Texture, Taste, Finish, Balance: _____

_____

Overall Assessment: _____

_____

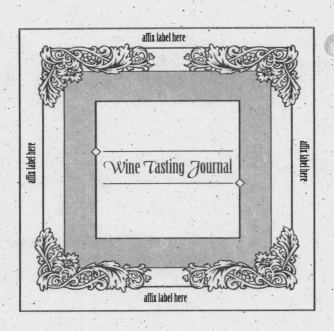

affix label here

affix label here

affix label here

affix label here

Wine Tasting Journal

Wine Record

◇

Name: _____

Producer: _____

Importer: _____

Grape Variety(ies): _____

Style/Region: _____ Vintage: _____

Date Purchased: _____ Country: _____

Purchase Price: _____ No. of bottles: _____

Purchased from: _____

Tasting Note

◇

Date opened: _____

Served with: _____

Guests: _____

Colour/Hue, Clarity: _____

_____

Aroma/Bouquet: _____

_____

Texture, Taste, Finish, Balance: _____

_____

Overall Assessment: _____

_____

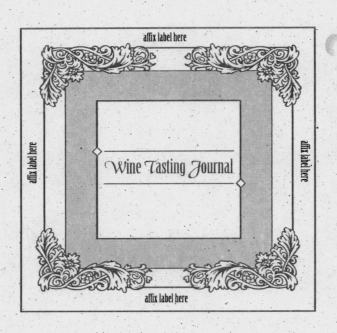

affix label here

affix label here

affix label here

affix label here

Wine Tasting Journal

Wine Record

Name: _____

Producer: _____

Importer: _____

Grape Variety(ies): _____

Style/Region: _____ Vintage: _____

Date Purchased: _____ Country: _____

Purchase Price: _____ No. of bottles: _____

Purchased from: _____

Tasting Note

Date opened: _____

Served with: _____

Guests: _____

Colour/Hue, Clarity: _____

_____

Aroma/Bouquet: _____

_____

Texture, Taste, Finish, Balance: _____

_____

Overall Assessment: _____

_____

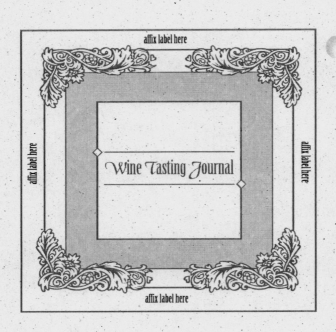

affix label here

affix label here

affix label here

affix label here

Wine Tasting Journal

Wine Record ◇

Name: _____

Producer: _____

Importer: _____

Grape Variety(ies): _____

Style/Region: _____ Vintage: _____

Date Purchased: _____ Country: _____

Purchase Price: _____ No. of bottles: _____

Purchased from: _____

Tasting Note ◇

Date opened: _____

Served with: _____

Guests: _____

Colour/Hue, Clarity: _____
_____

Aroma/Bouquet: _____
_____

Texture, Taste, Finish, Balance: _____
_____

Overall Assessment: _____
_____

affix label here

affix label here

affix label here

affix label here

Wine Tasting Journal

Wine Record

Name: _____

Producer: _____

Importer: _____

Grape Variety(ies): _____

Style/Region: _____ Vintage: _____

Date Purchased: _____ Country: _____

Purchase Price: _____ No. of bottles: _____

Purchased from: _____

Tasting Note

Date opened: _____

Served with: _____

Guests: _____

Colour/Hue, Clarity: _____

_____

Aroma/Bouquet: _____

_____

Texture, Taste, Finish, Balance: _____

_____

Overall Assessment: _____

_____

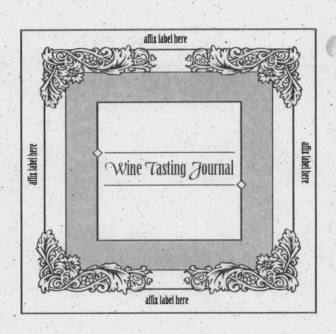

affix label here

affix label here

affix label here

affix label here

Wine Tasting Journal

Wine Record

◇

Name: _____

Producer: _____

Importer: _____

Grape Variety(ies): _____

Style/Region: _____ Vintage: _____

Date Purchased: _____ Country: _____

Purchase Price: _____ No. of bottles: _____

Purchased from: _____

Tasting Note

◇

Date opened: _____

Served with: _____

Guests: _____

Colour/Hue, Clarity: _____

_____

Aroma/Bouquet: _____

_____

Texture, Taste, Finish, Balance: _____

_____

Overall Assessment: _____

_____

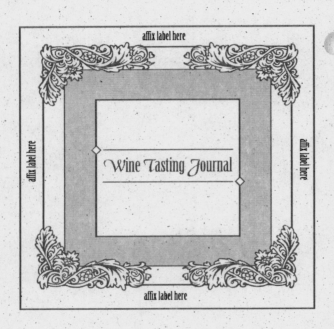

affix label here

affix label here

Wine Tasting Journal

affix label here

affix label here

Wine Record ◇

Name: _____

Producer: _____

Importer: _____

Grape Variety(ies): _____

Style/Region: _____ Vintage: _____

Date Purchased: _____ Country: _____

Purchase Price: _____ No. of bottles: _____

Purchased from: _____

Tasting Note ◇

Date opened: _____

Served with: _____

Guests: _____

Colour/Hue, Clarity: _____

_____

Aroma/Bouquet: _____

_____

Texture, Taste, Finish, Balance: _____

_____

Overall Assessment: _____

_____

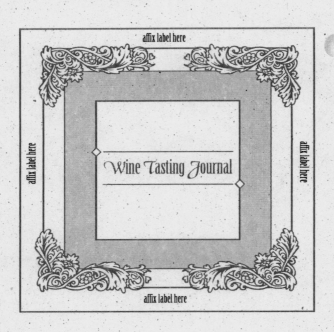

affix label here

affix label here

affix label here

Wine Tasting Journal

affix label here

Wine Record

Name: _____

Producer: _____

Importer: _____

Grape Variety(ies): _____

Style/Region: _____ Vintage: _____

Date Purchased: _____ Country: _____

Purchase Price: _____ No. of bottles: _____

Purchased from: _____

Tasting Note

Date opened: _____

Served with: _____

Guests: _____

Colour/Hue, Clarity: _____

_____

Aroma/Bouquet: _____

_____

Texture, Taste, Finish, Balance: _____

_____

Overall Assessment: _____

_____

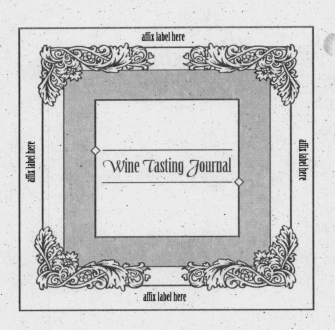

affix label here

affix label here

affix label here

Wine Tasting Journal

affix label here

Wine Record

◇

Name: _____

Producer: _____

Importer: _____

Grape Variety(ies): _____

Style/Region: _____ Vintage: _____

Date Purchased: _____ Country: _____

Purchase Price: _____ No. of bottles: _____

Purchased from: _____

Tasting Note

◇

Date opened: _____

Served with: _____

Guests: _____

Colour/Hue, Clarity: _____

_____

Aroma/Bouquet: _____

_____

Texture, Taste, Finish, Balance: _____

_____

Overall Assessment: _____

_____

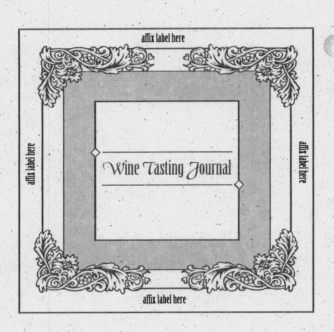

affix label here

affix label here

affix label here

Wine Tasting Journal

affix label here

Wine Record

◇

Name: _____

Producer: _____

Importer: _____

Grape Variety(ies): _____

Style/Region: _____ Vintage: _____

Date Purchased: _____ Country: _____

Purchase Price: _____ No. of bottles: _____

Purchased from: _____

Tasting Note

◇

Date opened: _____

Served with: _____

Guests: _____

Colour/Hue, Clarity: _____

_____

Aroma/Bouquet: _____

_____

Texture, Taste, Finish, Balance: _____

_____

Overall Assessment: _____

_____

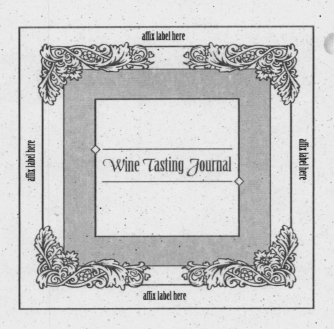

affix label here

affix label here

affix label here

Wine Tasting Journal

affix label here

Wine Record

◇

Name: _____

Producer: _____

Importer: _____

Grape Variety(ies): _____

Style/Region: _____ Vintage: _____

Date Purchased: _____ Country: _____

Purchase Price: _____ No. of bottles: _____

Purchased from: _____

Tasting Note

◇

Date opened: _____

Served with: _____

Guests: _____

Colour/Hue, Clarity: _____

_____

Aroma/Bouquet: _____

_____

Texture, Taste, Finish, Balance: _____

_____

Overall Assessment: _____

_____

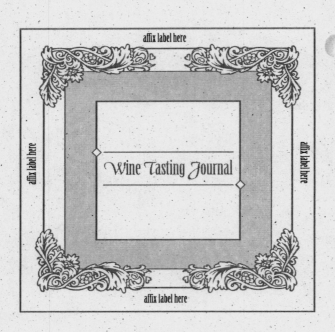

affix label here

affix label here

affix label here

affix label here

Wine Tasting Journal

Wine Record

◇

Name: _____

Producer: _____

Importer: _____

Grape Variety(ies): _____

Style/Region: _____ Vintage: _____

Date Purchased: _____ Country: _____

Purchase Price: _____ No. of bottles: _____

Purchased from: _____

Tasting Note

◇

Date opened: _____

Served with: _____

Guests: _____

Colour/Hue, Clarity: _____

_____

Aroma/Bouquet: _____

_____

Texture, Taste, Finish, Balance: _____

_____

Overall Assessment: _____

_____

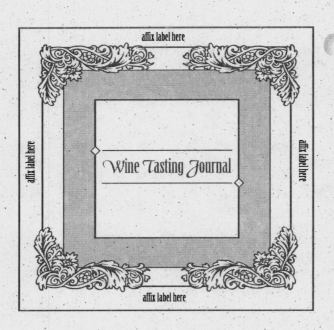

affix label here

affix label here

affix label here

Wine Tasting Journal

affix label here

Wine Record

◇

Name: _____

Producer: _____

Importer: _____

Grape Variety(ies): _____

Style/Region: _____ Vintage: _____

Date Purchased: _____ Country: _____

Purchase Price: _____ No. of bottles: _____

Purchased from: _____

Tasting Note

◇

Date opened: _____

Served with: _____

Guests: _____

Colour/Hue, Clarity: _____

_____

Aroma/Bouquet: _____

_____

Texture, Taste, Finish, Balance: _____

_____

Overall Assessment: _____

_____

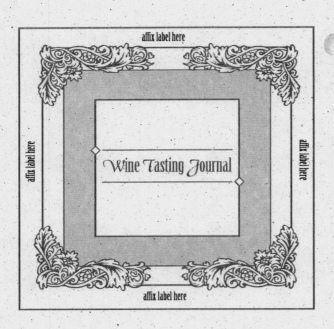

affix label here

affix label here

affix label here

Wine Tasting Journal

affix label here

Wine Record

Name: _____

Producer: _____

Importer: _____

Grape Variety(ies): _____

Style/Region: _____ Vintage: _____

Date Purchased: _____ Country: _____

Purchase Price: _____ No. of bottles: _____

Purchased from: _____

Tasting Note

Date opened: _____

Served with: _____

Guests: _____

Colour/Hue, Clarity: _____

_____

Aroma/Bouquet: _____

_____

Texture, Taste, Finish, Balance: _____

_____

Overall Assessment: _____

_____

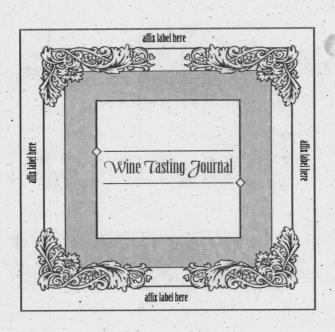

affix label here

affix label here

affix label here

affix label here

Wine Tasting Journal

Wine Record

◇

Name: _____

Producer: _____

Importer: _____

Grape Variety(ies): _____

Style/Region: _____ Vintage: _____

Date Purchased: _____ Country: _____

Purchase Price: _____ No. of bottles: _____

Purchased from: _____

Tasting Note

◇

Date opened: _____

Served with: _____

Guests: _____

Colour/Hue, Clarity: _____

_____

Aroma/Bouquet: _____

_____

Texture, Taste, Finish, Balance: _____

_____

Overall Assessment: _____

_____

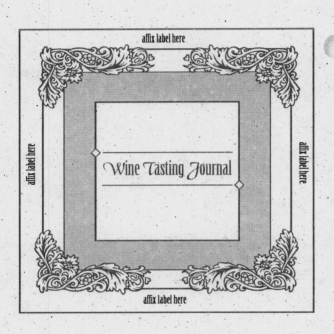

affix label here

affix label here

Wine Tasting Journal

affix label here

affix label here

Wine Record

◇

Name: _____

Producer: _____

Importer: _____

Grape Variety(ies): _____

Style/Region: _____ Vintage: _____

Date Purchased: _____ Country: _____

Purchase Price: _____ No. of bottles: _____

Purchased from: _____

Tasting Note

◇

Date opened: _____

Served with: _____

Guests: _____

Colour/Hue, Clarity: _____

_____

Aroma/Bouquet: _____

_____

Texture, Taste, Finish, Balance: _____

_____

Overall Assessment: _____

_____

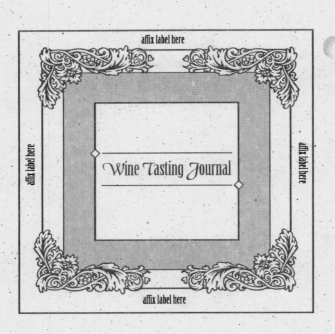

affix label here

affix label here

affix label here

Wine Tasting Journal

affix label here

Wine Record

Name: _____

Producer: _____

Importer: _____

Grape Variety(ies): _____

Style/Region: _____ Vintage: _____

Date Purchased: _____ Country: _____

Purchase Price: _____ No. of bottles: _____

Purchased from: _____

Tasting Note

Date opened: _____

Served with: _____

Guests: _____

Colour/Hue, Clarity: _____

_____

Aroma/Bouquet: _____

_____

Texture, Taste, Finish, Balance: _____

_____

Overall Assessment: _____

_____

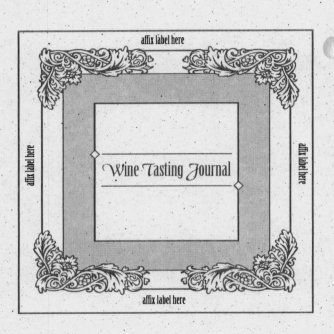

affix label here

affix label here

affix label here

affix label here

Wine Tasting Journal

Wine Record ◇

Name: _____

Producer: _____

Importer: _____

Grape Variety(ies): _____

Style/Region: _____ Vintage: _____

Date Purchased: _____ Country: _____

Purchase Price: _____ No. of bottles: _____

Purchased from: _____

Tasting Note ◇

Date opened: _____

Served with: _____

Guests: _____

Colour/Hue, Clarity: _____

_____

Aroma/Bouquet: _____

_____

Texture, Taste, Finish, Balance: _____

_____

Overall Assessment: _____

_____

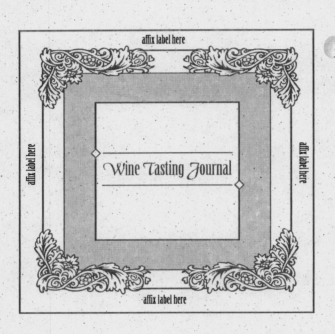

affix label here

affix label here

affix label here

Wine Tasting Journal

affix label here

Wine Record ◇

Name: _____

Producer: _____

Importer: _____

Grape Variety(ies): _____

Style/Region: _____ Vintage: _____

Date Purchased: _____ Country: _____

Purchase Price: _____ No. of bottles: _____

Purchased from: _____

Tasting Note ◇

Date opened: _____

Served with: _____

Guests: _____

Colour/Hue, Clarity: _____

_____

Aroma/Bouquet: _____

_____

Texture, Taste, Finish, Balance: _____

_____

Overall Assessment: _____

_____

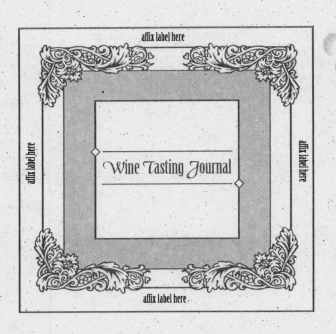

affix label here

affix label here

affix label here

affix label here

Wine Tasting Journal

Wine Record

◇

Name: _____

Producer: _____

Importer: _____

Grape Variety(ies): _____

Style/Region: _____ Vintage: _____

Date Purchased: _____ Country: _____

Purchase Price: _____ No. of bottles: _____

Purchased from: _____

Tasting Note

◇

Date opened: _____

Served with: _____

Guests: _____

Colour/Hue, Clarity: _____

_____

Aroma/Bouquet: _____

_____

Texture, Taste, Finish, Balance: _____

_____

Overall Assessment: _____

_____

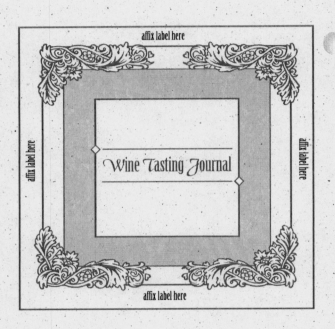

affix label here

affix label here

affix label here

affix label here

Wine Tasting Journal

Wine Record ◇

Name: _____

Producer: _____

Importer: _____

Grape Variety(ies): _____

Style/Region: _____ Vintage: _____

Date Purchased: _____ Country: _____

Purchase Price: _____ No. of bottles: _____

Purchased from: _____

Tasting Note ◇

Date opened: _____

Served with: _____

Guests: _____

Colour/Hue, Clarity: _____

_____

Aroma/Bouquet: _____

_____

Texture, Taste, Finish, Balance: _____

_____

Overall Assessment: _____

_____

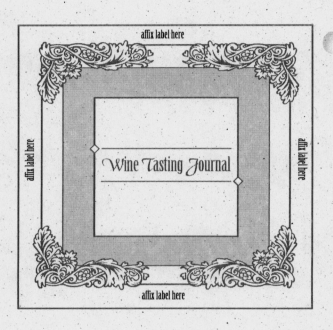

affix label here

affix label here

affix label here

Wine Tasting Journal

affix label here

Wine Record ◇

Name: _____

Producer: _____

Importer: _____

Grape Variety(ies): _____

Style/Region: _____ Vintage: _____

Date Purchased: _____ Country: _____

Purchase Price: _____ No. of bottles: _____

Purchased from: _____

Tasting Note ◇

Date opened: _____

Served with: _____

Guests: _____

Colour/Hue, Clarity: _____

_____

Aroma/Bouquet: _____

_____

Texture, Taste, Finish, Balance: _____

_____

Overall Assessment: _____

_____

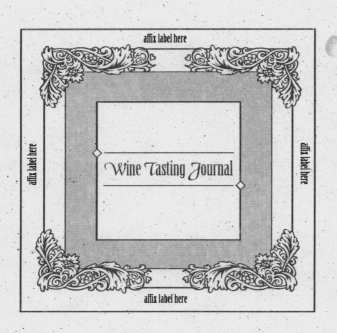

affix label here

affix label here

affix label here

affix label here

Wine Tasting Journal

Wine Record

◇

Name: _____

Producer: _____

Importer: _____

Grape Variety(ies): _____

Style/Region: _____ Vintage: _____

Date Purchased: _____ Country: _____

Purchase Price: _____ No. of bottles: _____

Purchased from: _____

Tasting Note

◇

Date opened: _____

Served with: _____

Guests: _____

Colour/Hue, Clarity: _____

_____

Aroma/Bouquet: _____

_____

Texture, Taste, Finish, Balance: _____

_____

Overall Assessment: _____

_____

affix label here

affix label here

affix label here

affix label here

Wine Tasting Journal

Wine Record

Name: _____

Producer: _____

Importer: _____

Grape Variety(ies): _____

Style/Region: _____ Vintage: _____

Date Purchased: _____ Country: _____

Purchase Price: _____ No. of bottles: _____

Purchased from: _____

Tasting Note

Date opened: _____

Served with: _____

Guests: _____

Colour/Hue, Clarity: _____

_____

Aroma/Bouquet: _____

_____

Texture, Taste, Finish, Balance: _____

_____

Overall Assessment: _____

_____

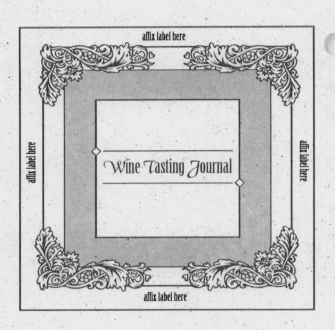

affix label here

affix label here

affix label here

affix label here

Wine Tasting Journal

Wine Record

Name: _____

Producer: _____

Importer: _____

Grape Variety(ies): _____

Style/Region: _____ Vintage: _____

Date Purchased: _____ Country: _____

Purchase Price: _____ No. of bottles: _____

Purchased from: _____

Tasting Note

Date opened: _____

Served with: _____

Guests: _____

Colour/Hue, Clarity: _____

_____

Aroma/Bouquet: _____

_____

Texture, Taste, Finish, Balance: _____

_____

Overall Assessment: _____

_____

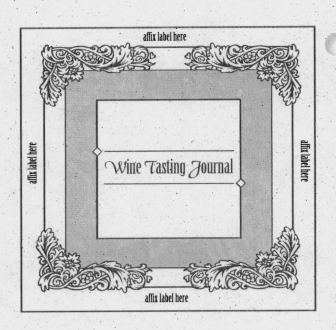

affix label here

affix label here

affix label here

affix label here

Wine Tasting Journal

Wine Record ◇

Name: _____

Producer: _____

Importer: _____

Grape Variety(ies): _____

Style/Region: _____ Vintage: _____

Date Purchased: _____ Country: _____

Purchase Price: _____ No. of bottles: _____

Purchased from: _____

Tasting Note ◇

Date opened: _____

Served with: _____

Guests: _____

Colour/Hue, Clarity: _____

_____

Aroma/Bouquet: _____

_____

Texture, Taste, Finish, Balance: _____

_____

Overall Assessment: _____

_____